The Mouse Stone

Written by Andrew Melrose

Illustrated by George Hollingworth

Annie was playing in her garden, when she spotted something very strange.

"What is it?" shouted Billy.

"Sh!" whispered Annie. "You will frighten it."

Billy climbed over his garden fence to take a closer look.

"Frighten what?" he whispered in his softest voice.

Annie pointed to a large rock. At the bottom there was a small hole. It was about the size of a plum.

Billy peered into the hole. Then suddenly he shouted again, "IT'S A MOUSE!"

"Sh!" said Annie again.

"Sorry," whispered Billy.

Meera from next door heard Billy shouting and came round.

"It's a mouse in a hole," whispered Billy.

"Can't he get out?" Meera asked.

"No," replied Annie, "he's too fat!"

"Oh, the poor thing," replied Meera.

Billy smiled, "I could give him a poke with this stick!"

"No," said Annie. "You'll frighten him."

But Meera was puzzled.

"Annie," she said, "if the mouse is too fat to get out of the hole, how did he get in?"

"It's very simple, really," said Annie. "He's a very greedy mouse. After our party tea last week, he waited until everyone had gone to bed. Then he came looking for the leftover food."

"I didn't know there were any leftovers," Billy said. He usually liked to fill a party bag to take home.

"But the mouse knew about the leftovers!" Annie smiled.

"He found two sandwiches, a squashed piece of chocolate cake, half a juicy apple, and some wobbly raspberry jelly. He carried them, one by one, into his hole."

Billy loved jelly. He wondered how the little mouse managed to carry the wobbly jelly back to his hole.

"What did he do with all the food?" asked Meera. "I can't see any now."

"He had a feast, of course," laughed Annie. "First he ate the sandwiches…

...then the squashy piece of chocolate cake...

...then he ate the juicy apple, pips and all."

"Yuck, pips!" said Billy.

"And last of all, he ate the wobbly raspberry jelly."

"Oh!" sighed Billy. Raspberry was his favourite.

"But I still don't understand how he got stuck in the hole," said Meera.

"Oh, that's easy," replied Annie. "Eating all that party food made him too fat to get out!"

Now Meera was worried. "But Annie, the party tea was last week. Won't the little mouse be getting hungry by now?"

"I expect so," replied Annie.

Meera frowned. "Poor little mouse," she said.

"I have a leftover chewy toffee," said Billy. "I've been saving it. We could feed it to him."

"And I have an apple core," added Meera. "I could fetch it."

"No," said Annie. "If we feed the little mouse more food, he will stay fat. He could be stuck in the hole forever."

"What can we do?" asked Meera.

Annie wasn't sure. She was worried that the little mouse might be hungry. But she didn't want him to be stuck for ever.

They all thought very hard.

Then Billy began to push his sticky toffee into the hole.

"STOP!" shouted Annie.

Billy got such a fright that he tumbled over.

Meera ran forward and tried to grab him, but they both fell, knocking over the rock.

"Oh no!" gasped everyone, as the rock rolled away.

Annie, Meera and Billy stared in amazement.

"That's not a mouse!" shouted Billy.

"It's just a little stone that looks like a mouse!" added Meera.

"Hah! Fooled you all," shouted Annie. She was pretending she had known all along.

Now Billy was puzzled. "I wonder what a little mouse stone did with all that party food?"